Pushing Through The Pain

PUSHING *Through* THE PAIN

How I made it through

Author
DENEATRICE MILLNER

XULON PRESS

Xulon Press
2301 Lucien Way #415
Maitland, FL 32751
407.339.4217
www.xulonpress.com

© 2018 by Deneatrice Millner

All rights reserved solely by the author. The author guarantees all contents are original and do not infringe upon the legal rights of any other person or work. No part of this book may be reproduced in any form without the permission of the author. The views expressed in this book are not necessarily those of the publisher.

Scripture quotations taken from the Holy Bible, New International Version (NIV). Copyright © 1973, 1978, 1984, 2011 by Biblica, Inc.™. Used by permission. All rights reserved.

Printed in the United States of America.

ISBN-13: 9781545653500

Contents

Introduction ix

Chapter One: Why So Much Pain? 1

Chapter Two: Emotional Trauma 14

Chapter Three: Rejection and Validation 35

Chapter Four: Stuffing the Pain 48

Chapter Five: Pain of Addictions 64

Chapter Six: Broken Relationships 80

Chapter Seven: Just Deal with It 87

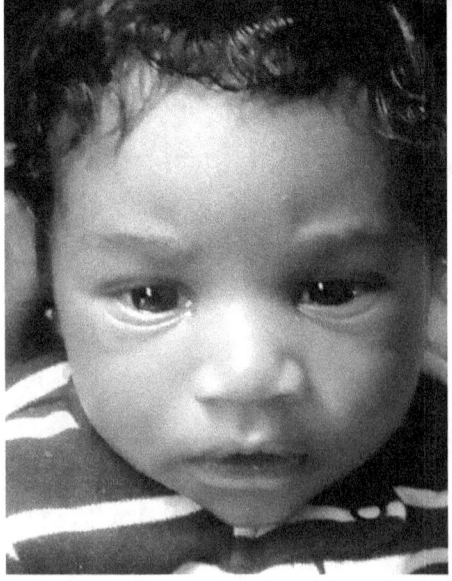

Introduction

Four years ago *Pushing through the Pain* was given to me to write about, and I finally got the courage to do it. When writing about pain, I found myself healing in areas I thought I was free from, but I learned pushing problems away doesn't always mean you are over it. We've all heard, "Just get over it," right? It's not always that easy.

In writing about pain and being open, I hope it helps you understand the depth of it and how important it is to overcome and have victory over the problems you can't handle. It is important to trust God to guide you to a healthy more peaceful way to handle your situations, whether they are from your childhood or an adult..

I experienced a lot of abandonment issues that stemmed from my childhood, as well as abuse from my mother, and low self-esteem because I was told that I would never be anything in life by family I thought that really loved me. Having to deal with those issues, I recognized the damage it had done to me and how I battled to come out.

I'll address the pain of rejection, which goes with our need for validation. These two go hand in hand, because if you ever find yourself feeling rejected you'll also find the need of validation right behind it. There are many things people deal with that cause so much pain and instead of facing it, they stuff it, like I did, and pretend it isn't there. I will also talk about the addictions and broken relationships I experienced. Lastly, I will speak about how to just deal with you and how dealing with me changed my life.

We are like the man who laid at the pool for thirty-eight years, as written in John 5. When Jesus saw him lying there and learned he had been in this condition for a long time, He asked him, "Do you want to get well?" (John 5:6). Let's talk about this place where this man laid, first in John 5:2 it was in Jerusalem near the Sheep Gate a pool, which in Aramaic is called Bethesda ,which was surrounded by five covered colonnades. These colonnades are a set of pillars holding up a canopy. The people who were disabled laid there waiting to get in the pool when the water was stirred. This man laid here for 38 years and I'm sure there were people that seen him in that condition that walked by and didn't help him. He was not able to walk so there was no way he could beat other people to the pool and no one helped him. I thought on this and as I read how Jesus talked to him out of all the people, I noticed there was no judgment of how long he been there he just wanted to see him get well. He asked him what he wanted first, because God don't go against your will and when the man answered then he helped him. How many times we judge people because of how long they've been in a painful situation, and not just helped or how many times have we judged our own selves and it caused us to get stuck in that situation.

I'm sure that's the same question He asks us when we are in pain. Do we want to get well? We may say yes, but what do we do about it?

John 5:7 says, "He replied, 'Sir, I have no one to help me into the pool when the water is stirred.'" He also says, "While I am trying to get in, someone else goes down ahead of me."

This is the way it was for me—I stayed feeling sorry for myself and helpless. I was just like that man: paralyzed, stuck in my situation, not knowing how to get out. I knew people who seen me in some painful situations but left me in it. I blamed everyone else for my hurt. I didn't know how to accept people treating me the same way I treated myself. I could have "stepped in the water" when I felt that pain, but instead I sat in pity, wanting others to help me when I needed to use my own faith to help myself. I could have done it earlier, but I let pain bound me to pity, and low self-esteem, from being told I would never amount to anything and I was never encouraged to go forward in my singing which is a gift that God has given me. I didn't have the support in singing and I knew that when I would sing I felt free from all of my problems I had.

Will you pick up your bed and walk, or will you stay in your painful state? I hope through reading my story, it will help you make a decision to push through your pain and get up and walk with me, because you can be victorious over any of your problems.

Chapter One

Why So Much Pain?

I've always wondered why people suffer. Why there is so much pain. I know I'm not the only one who feels like this.

I believe in God, so I read the Bible and found in Genesis 2:15, which states that God put Adam in the Garden of Eden, where there was no pain only peace. It was never God's plan for us to experience all this pain. His original plans were for us to live in paradise with him forever. Ecclesiastes 3:10–11 says, "I have seen the occupation that God has given to the sons of men to keep them occupied. He has made everything beautiful in its time. He has even put eternity in their heart; yet mankind will never find out the work that the true God has made from start to finish." Even if you may say, "I don't believe in the Bible," I understand because we all have doubted God at some point in our lives, but here's what I can say to that.

In the book of Genesis, in the beginning, God spoke everything into existence, including Adam and Eve. Genesis 2:7 states, "Then the Lord God formed a man from the dust of the ground and breathed into his nostrils the breath of life and the man became a living being." Isn't it amazing how the only creation God ever breathe in was us. He put his Spirit in us. Genesis 2:22 states, "Then the Lord God made a woman from the rib he had taken out of the man, and he brought her to the man."

Adam and Eve lived a good life in the garden where there was no sin or pain. They were even naked, according to Genesis 2:25, "Adam and his wife were both naked, and they felt no shame." They had no reason to feel anything but happiness. They experienced no sin or sorrow, nor misery. God made Adam and Eve's lives pleasant, all they had to do was tend to the garden, and they were in paradise until they made the decision to disobey. God gave Adam a commandment in Genesis 2:16-17: "You are free to eat from any tree in the garden, but you must not eat from the knowledge of good and evil, for when you eat from it, you will certainly die."

How many times have we been warned about something and haven't heeded to that warning? That's exactly what Adam did.

Adam didn't listen to God, because if he had listened to God it would have prompted obedience; he would have remembered the word of God when he said, "You will surely die." Adam wouldn't have eaten that fruit. There's no way he would have chosen death or pain. He had everything and lost it all by listening to his wife and not God. Adam didn't stand on the words of God and instead helped Eve in her disobedience and went along with her.

Through their disobedience, pain and sin came to the world. Genesis 3:16 To the woman he said, " I will make your pains in childbearing very severe with painful labor you will give birth to children." One thing about God is He doesn't allow excuses. He likes us to take responsibility for our actions—own our sins—and admit we've done wrong. We have to remember every day we are given free will to make a decision on our lives, we are responsible at that moment of what we decide to do when the opportunity come for us to do what's right. Once we are told the right from the wrong we are then responsible for that decision we have made no one else will take the fall for us before God. From Adam and Eve's disobedience came death. In Genesis 2:16–17, God shows us that obedience and responsibility are important to Him.

Our God is direct. He first made everything by His mouth: He spoke and something appeared. He made Adam to watch over the garden. Yes, God trusted him. He had to believe in Adam or He wouldn't have given the garden to him.

Maybe your next question is, "Didn't God already knows Adam would fall?" Sure he did, but God, because of who He is, gave Adam the free will to obey. God doesn't command that everyone should obey Him. Genesis 1:26 states, "Then God said, 'Let us make mankind in our image, in our likeness, so they may rule.'"

He made male and female. He didn't make us so we would fall or suffer; God had a plan for mankind when he placed Adam and Eve in paradise to live with him forever and prosper, just like He still has a plan today for us to live with him forever and to prosper and be in good health.

Think about yourself for a moment. Do you rebel or get angry when you are told what to do? Are you stubborn? Are you like Adam and Eve and do what you want, even when God gives you instructions to do something else? Do you blame others for your situations or the pain in your life?

Adam fell from grace because of whom he chose to listen. To whom are you listening? Are you like Eve who listened to the serpent when she knew she wasn't supposed to listen to him? Nothing happened until Adam disobeyed and ate the fruit. Why? Because God spoke with Adam first, giving him the commandment.. Usually, when there's disobedience, there's pain.

There was one tree of good and one of evil in the garden. Once Adam and Eve messed with evil, pain came into existence. A lot of us do that today — we want to see what it's like to do what we want. When we do things our own way, it feels like everything is okay until the bottom falls out from underneath us. There have been many times I didn't listen, my spiritual dad used to tell me to stop listening to women gossip because they were only trying to pull me in it. I wanted to be liked so much that I didn't take heed and found myself in mess in the church. If I had listened to my mentor, I wouldn't have been caught up in the mess. Gossip is like a murderer, it kills someone's character, and I was guilty because I listened to the women. At the time I was doing it I was making friends I thought, I felt like I was being blessed because everything was going good for me. My ex-husband and I got a new car and moved into a new apartment, I thought for sure I was really blessed, then the Lord showed me he had mercy on me but it does not mean you won't suffer for the wrong that you do. I'm saying don't confused things with blessings because God judges our character and our attitudes toward others. I did suffer for allowing my ears to be a garbage can to peoples mess. They were able to dump their mess in my can, which was my ears and let me say this you reap what you sow. People talked about me and no one stood up for me that's when I learned my lesson for being partaker in someone else's wrong doings. The devil is cunning with us just like he was with Eve—present sin to us and we fall for the lies. We know better; we know we are not supposed to, but we do it anyway—trying to please our flesh. James 1:14 says, "But each person is tempted when they are dragged away by their own evil desire and enticed. Then, after desire has conceived, it gives birth to sin; and sin, when it is full-grown, gives birth to death. "

Have you ever heard the phrase, "Do what makes you happy"? Don't fall for that one because everything you think will make you happy is not always right. So I say, "Do what *God* says." He knows what's best. He knows you, and He has plans for your life. People also say, "Everything that looks good is not good," and that, I agree with.

We are tempted every day to go left; it's a daily fight to choose to do what's right. 1 Corinthians 10:23 Paul says, " I have the right to do anything," you say but not everything is good for you." Things are presented to us, just like Eve presented the fruit to Adam.

Is there someone presenting something to you in your life today that God commanded you not to do? It doesn't have to be a person; it could be the devil pressuring you to do something that you know is wrong because you are lured by your own lustful desires. Fornication, which is having sex without marriage is a sin you do against your own body because as a Christian, when you do this, you are taking your own body and degrading it, defiling it or uniting it with a prostitute. It also brings on diseases to your body that is a consequence for the sin. 1 Corinthians 6:13 says, "The body is not meant for sexual immorality but for the Lord and the Lord for the body." 1 Corinthians 6:15 states, "Do you not know that your bodies are members of Christ himself? Shall I then take the members of Christ and unite them with a prostitute?" But there are other temptations and addictions like alcohol, drugs, and food, which are more of an act of putting it in your body instead of using your body to join your soul with someone else's soul.

We go to these things because they immediately act as medication to numb our pain. We'll talk more on addiction later, but we have to understand the enemy uses these devices to bound us and make us feel like it will help us more than God. Yet, it's all a deception.

Why do we go to these things instead of God? Paul says it best in Romans 7:21 (NIV), which states, "So I find this law at work: Although I want to do good, evil is right there with me The flesh wants to do what it wants, and as long as we walk in it, we are an enemy to God. Why? Because God is a Spirit and when you worship Him, it has to be done in the Spirit. The desires of the flesh go against God, and it does not want to obey God.

So, pain came to Adam and Eve through their disobedience to God, separating them from God. When we go through our pain and we don't listen, the moment we choose to be disobedient, it separates us from God. Sometimes when we are in pain we get mad at God because we feel we shouldn't be going through that situation at that time. We all do the Why me Lord? The moment we decide to rebell because of the circumstance is the moment we allow sin to control us. Sin separates us because when we choose to do what we want and not acknowledge God for who He is or consult Him about our decisions, we are not being obedient. At that moment, when we say, "I'm going to do it this way," and not at least pray before we do it, or follow the Spirit, or, say "I had a feeling to do this," God wants to reach us to guide us to the right way—His way—we have to give up our will and submit to do it.

I remember when I was younger I dreamed that the man I was seeing was cheating on me with someone close to me. The Lord warned me in a dream and told me not to go see him. I did it anyway. God knew I would sleep with him so he warned me, but I did what I wanted and I opened the door to pain and brought shame to myself, and wanted to blame God but I couldn't. We blame God because we want what we want and when He doesn't step in the way and allows something to go wrong—and it normally does—we get mad and angry about it. Then we blame God and say, "Why didn't you stop this? Why did you let this happen?"

I want to ask you why *you* let this happen. It was your choice and no one made you do it; you decided it was what you wanted, but it didn't turn out right. I decided I wanted that man, my low self-esteem, and insecurities was in the way of my decision to do what was right. I was also trying to prove to God I was strong and was weak as water. It's better to obey God if you don't you leave a door open.

Then we can't close the door because it's wide open for the enemy to come in and have his way in our lives.

I have learned to close all the doors in my life so the enemy can't slip in. One way to do this is through the mouth. The Bible says in Proverbs 18:21 (NIV), "The tongue has the power of life and death, and those who love it will eat its fruit." I always opened the door through speaking negative things about myself and about my situations. Even though I knew the scripture when I was in pain, I would say, "I'm not no good," "I'm stupid" or "nobody loves me," until I realized my life was headed downhill by speaking bad things about myself. I was too scared to think anything else of myself because I didn't feel worth anything. If any relationship I was in wasn't going the way I wanted it, I would speak against the relationship. My words caused destruction to myself and my relationships with others.

There are many times we have opened doors out of pain because we haven't properly dealt with it and this can cause us to have bitterness. Oh bitterness is a bad thing to have in your heart, and I had it there from being angry, disappointed and feeling I wasn't treated fairly in life. I remember I was so mad at God for what I went through I didn't want to pray, I didn't want to talk to him because it seemed it was one battle after another. I would go through in my marriage, then the car would break down or we didn't have enough money it was always something. As time went on and I grew in the word I realized that those things wasn't there to kill me only to make me stronger in my faith. I had to look at pain in a different way than I was because my attitude towards my life became bad and I had to change. Sometimes, we justify our feelings and we use them for our protection from being hurt again. For example, I was married before and when I held onto the pain that I felt from that marriage I was able to justify using anger to protect myself from getting hurt again.

I realize that it was just an excuse to not let the anger go because I was comfortable protecting myself and not allowing God to be my protection.

When you hold onto your pain, its results can be fatal. Take for instance, obesity, which is a real problem in America today. I know because that's one of my struggles, but I'm going to beat it because as I'm writing this book, I'm working on losing the forty pounds I have left. It is estimated that 75 percent of overeating is caused by emotions. A nutritionist, Joy Bauer, was invited on the *Today* show. She said stress, anxiety, sadness, boredom, anger, loneliness, relationship problems, and poor self-esteem can all trigger emotional eating, so people overeat because of their emotions or pain, making them overweight. Even though I see someone with five hundred extra pounds, it's no different than my forty pounds because it's still considered obese and likely the result of hidden pain within that person.

Pushing through pain isn't easy, but I will tell you my story of how I pushed through painful situations, and made it to the other side of that pain. So, let's push.

Chapter Two

Emotional Trauma

I thought, at least until I started going to school, my life was no different than any other child. I had a big family: my mother had twelve children. She told me about having two miscarriages and one stillborn. She told me about the miscarriages when I was married to my first husband. She never went into details of the miscarriages, but we had to know her medical history because I was pregnant with my first child at the time. She'd had the miscarriages before I was born, but when she had the stillbirth I was a teenager. One night, my mother went into every room looking to see if her family was okay because she felt someone was dead. She later found out when she went to the hospital that baby Theresa was dead inside of her. I felt hurt and saddened because the baby was full term and we expected to see her. When she didn't come home we were heartbroken. My dad was so hurt, he told us when he got home and said he had to make a decision between my mom and the child. He chose my mom. My mom had developed diabetes and it killed the child. This, of course, hurt them both so bad. My dad cried and my mom talked about her for a day or two, but never mentioned her again. We went on with our lives, and they later had two more kids before they called off the marriage.

So much happened in our house all the time, there were times we laughed and times we cried together. We played games a lot, especially when my parents would go on dates. My brothers would run through the house. I remember there was this song called, "What Ever It Is" by James Cleveland and one of my brother's was so caught up in the song that he jumped on the table and it collapsed. We all looked like we were all in trouble, because, with our parents, if one child did something bad and tried to hide it we all got whipped. So, we all got together and fixed the table before our parents came home.

When I went to school, I was teased for wearing long skirts and dresses all the time. We couldn't wear pants at that time, because of our religion and other kids looked at me and laughed, like something was wrong with me. My mom and dad took us to a Pentecostal church that taught women weren't allowed to wear pants. I dreaded going to school for that reason. The children were mean and didn't care about what they said that would hurt you. Sometimes all I could do was just pray to God for help. I had to deal with what was going on at home which was abuse and alcoholism, then go to school and be teased by children I didn't even know. I didn't want to be bitter in life so I took advantage of going to church because it was the only out I had. Teachers also noticed my mom was pregnant all the time. They always asked me questions, like "How many children does your mom have?" and if I answered, I got in trouble with my mom. The teachers would say something to her about it, my mom would smack me and tell me, "You talk too much," but no one ever told me not

Emotional Trauma

to talk. How could I not answer them? Her belly was so huge, so often, hardly anyone missed it. What she didn't know was I suffered at school because we went to church all the time and we dressed different from other kids.

It felt like my sisters and brothers didn't have the same issues at school. I was the seventh child and alone all the time because it was a lot for my mom to deal with being married and being abused, while trying to raise us and I required more attention which she could't give.

No one at home talked about my discomfort but one of my older brothers who would stand up to my mom when she would hit me and tell her to hit him instead he was and still is my protector. We weren't allowed to express any feelings; we never had sit down discussions unless we got in trouble. We were also told to "Be quiet," so we did what we knew best to do: shut up and keep moving forward, and that's when I realized my voice didn't count if I spoke no one would listen.

My first trauma came when I was about seven or eight years old, right before we went to church. My parents got into a fight, but that time was different. I remember seeing my dad beat my mom so bad that she fell on my older brother who was fourteen years old. She screamed for help. I stood in the bedroom door, helpless, not knowing what to do. My dad later decided to leave the house.

When my dad drank, his behavior would become erratic. So, in order for them to survive their marriage, my parents started going to church. At the time I thought *what kind of church is this?* In addition to wearing dresses or skirts all the time, we weren't allowed to watch TV or listen to the radio because the church said that would allow the devil to control our house. Also, the church didn't believe in birth control because the scripture says in Genesis 1:28, "God blessed them and said to them, 'Be fruitful and increase in number, fill the earth and subdue it.'" So the church used that scripture to say it was wrong to use birth control to stop God's creation. I'm not against having kids I now have eight and never regretted having any of them, but this scripture does not just speak for us to multiply in children, but in every area of our lives we should be fruitful. He also wants us to increase or to enlarge, I believe God wants us to be skillful in our gifts and grow in our gifts where we not only benefit financially from it but it also gives God total glory in your life. When we take our gifts and multiply it we are not only being wise but we are showing how to go in the world and reproduce what God has given us and give to others also. Most people would give up when it comes to experiencing this kind of restriction from a church, it can detour you from God if you let it I can't say it did not affect me because it did when it came to trusting pastors. I watched Pastors throughout my life in the church being controlling, and operating in witchcraft, being deceptive and lying. After experiencing this it did not push me away from God but made me want to know him more. I said within myself I don't want to be like them, it was scary to see people in positions and abuse it. I realize that being a leader takes discipline and I didn't know all I had to do in Christ, but I did know that leadership took great responsibility. It also takes wisdom and knowledge, to do any job especially God's call on your life, and if you don't do it with wisdom and knowledge you will fail. I didn't know who I was to be a great leader, I know now that you have to have confidence in God as a leader and you have to be willing to sacrifice you carnal nature to become spiritual in God's kingdom. This has kept me focused on doing God's will and not allowing other people's mistakes to steer me in the wrong direction. There are great leaders and churches out there please don't stay home and sit down on God over a man's flaws. I want to encourage you to keep your eyes on God when you up under leadership and always pray for your leaders they have struggles too, make sure you are up under a real leader one who will own his or her mistakes and change their ways. I'm saying this because my dad is also a preacher and battled alcoholism before he went into the ministry, I seen him preach and live what he knew, but I also seen him not do all God had called him to do, but that's between him and God. Our family was known as a church family in the community so everyone knew us...

At school, my mom was popular because my last two sisters were eleven and twelve pounds when they were born and back in the 80s it was a big deal to survive that, and she did. She was even in the newspaper. After my two sisters were born, I felt like I was noticed even less. My mom stayed busy with everything else and when life showed up for me, which means problems at school, dealing with bullying, feeling depressed, and feeling alone, I had to figure it out myself.

My mom became depressed and mean sometimes. She would stay in bed for days or get mad over small things and scream through the house. She would bite her finger because the stress was so much for her that she needed an out and that was her way. We also knew somebody was about to get hit with her fist when she bit her finger. My mom never recovered from the diabetes she gained during pregnancy, so I didn't know all that she dealt with when it came to that disease but I knew she wasn't well. My sister and I would have to give her shots to manage her diabetes. It was very hard to have to stick a needle in her leg or arm but my mom needed it to live.

I also noticed the mental state my mom was in because of the diabetes. If she didn't eat just right, the disease affected the way she thought, and she was very stubborn when it came to her dietary restrictions. My mom would go to the doctor and he would have her admitted to the hospital because her blood pressure had spiked.

My mom and dad still saw each other, which was confusing as a thirteen year old girl. They always went back and forth about their relationship. One day they would be flirting and the next they wouldn't speak.

One day, my dad must have told her he wasn't seeing another woman anymore, and my mom decided to drive by where she thought he might be with the other woman, and she took my sister and me with her. When she got there, we saw my dad and the other woman together sitting at the restaurant eating. My mom went ballistic. She was extremely angry and screamed at both of them. I stood outside and tried to calm her down by telling her it would be okay. Then she looked toward heaven and said, "You did this to me," to God.

I couldn't believe it. I thought *will God forgive her for what she said*? She told Him she hated Him.

I know we've all been there, maybe some more than others—the blame game of "This is why my life is like this. You, God, you made this happen." My mother was angry at God for her decisions. She didn't have to stay with my father or keep dealing with his abuse and cheating; it was her choice. I say that because she knew he was having an affair and instead of walking away, she stayed with him.

I was so hurt because I loved God with everything in me and I knew she was hurt when she spoke to God like that. I never blamed God for seeing my Dad and Mom in that position I knew that once you let the enemy in a little he'll take control and that was done to their marriage.

I know it was a difficult time for my mother, but I also know, she knew how my dad was and she thought he would change for her, I believe she got a woman's intuition because she would talk about the feeling she would get when something was wrong, and she wasn't paying attention to the signs. I think she wanted my father at any cost. I watched how she was with my dad and how she would fight with him when she couldn't get his attention. It was hard to deal with because I thought he was just mean to her and it affected the way I was with him or any man. I watched my mother become emotionally out of control and didn't know her behavior would soon become my behavior. I watched her allow her emotions control her and then, as I grew, I was not able to handle some pain as well. Rejection was the hardest pain for me to overcome. I know now, I became my mother even though I hadn't wanted to. I hated the way she was so angry, resentful, depressed, unhappy, and negative, which is what her pain did to her through not wanting to deal with it.

My mother's pain was a weapon she used to protect herself from people. The people she trusted let her down, and the pain she carried from that was her defense.

It is common to see people using pain as a shield. No one can get through to them because their pain runs so deep inside of them.

We all need to face our own pain and not allow it to control us to the point that we make people afraid to come near us. Some people are so hurt that they are numb to life, and because that pain controls their every decision, they get stuck. That was me.

I was stuck because I held onto the pain. I never fit in at school or with my own family. I didn't understand why God put me on earth. I was so lost as a person in which direction my life was going because my dad was gone and my family was completely torn apart I know that identity comes from family and I was totally confused on who I was because there was no stability anymore in the house. My mom started beating me, more and more when I was about fourteen years old. When she got mad at my dad, she would take her anger out on me instead. My mom knew how much I loved my dad, so she got mad when I wanted to be around him. I hated myself more when she would beat me because I had no knowledge that my identity did not rely on how my mother felt about me. She would try to hit my sister but one day my sister kicked her in the stomach, after that my mother appeared to be afraid of her. I continued to fear when my mother would hit me and grab my hair. I didn't have anyone but God to share my hurt. I wanted my mom to love me, to hug me, and encourage me. I couldn't get why she didn't want to love me. I couldn't comprehend why, out of all her kids, she would beat me. My mom would just hit me, I mean when she would walk by me I would jump because she would just smack me out of no where

I felt like a woman who was around a man she loved and when she made him mad, he slapped her so hard she would fall to the floor. It's a bad thing to be around someone and never know when they will hit you. I would live in fear of her that she would be upset about something that reminded her of my dad and beat me. That's a bad feeling as a child when you are torn between your parents because you love them both but they have you in the middle of their confusion. Sometimes I found myself siding with one to get their love and feeling guilty because you want both to love you or sometimes as a child I felt like I was the reason they broke up.

Some days were better than others. I recall a day I wanted to go to church with my friend. I was so excited because I heard about the Holy Ghost and I wanted him so bad I was willing to risk my life to find him, I heard he could change my life, me and my mom talked about my friend calling me at 8:00 am to wake me up and make sure I am ready. She seemed happy that I was going to church too, so I got my clothes out the night before. I woke up Sunday morning and waited, wondering why my friend hadn't called. I asked my mom, but she ignored me. Then, I noticed the phone was off the hook. She actually took the phone off the hook so I could not go to church. I confronted her in respect but asked, "Did the girl call?" I knew what my mom did, but I needed Jesus. That day, I was willing to go through anything to get to Him. My mom got mad because she knew what she had done. I believe my mom knew what she was doing. That day she came at me and grabbed me, and when she did, she was in front of the stairs. I heard an evil voice say, "Push her down the stairs." But I couldn't do it. I got around her to go down the stairs and she grabbed me by the hair. I literally hung off the stairs. I don't know how I got away. I remember saying to my mom, "Somebody has to go to church in this family. There's evil in here." I was willing to go through that pain to get to Jesus because He was the only one who could get me out of my situations.

There was a time when I was fifteen years old, that I was a seer. I saw a lot in dreams, and one day, I saw my sister was pregnant, about five months along I think. I remember telling her about the dream and she started counting on her fingers. I stood there watching her count and wondered if she was actually pregnant. My mom was so angry when she found out my sister was pregnant. In my dream, I saw my sister sitting at the table in a blue short jumper trying to explain herself. That's exactly the way it went when it actually happened. My mom was angry and she later asked me if I knew. I told her I had seen it in a dream. Then she asked, "How many months is she?" So I told her. Then she got mad and beat me, as though *I* was the one who was pregnant.

I asked, "Why are you hitting me?"

She said, "There was no way you could have known that by a dream. She had to have told you."

"No, she didn't tell me."

My gift has always been a problem for people close to me because they appeared to think something is wrong with me. It started with my mother and the way she treated me when I was being myself. I remember the way she looked at me when I was happy, I could be dancing she would look at me like she didn't like me or when I would get dressed up she would look like I was dressed like a fast girl, back then it was not a good name to be called fast. My mom use to say I was fast and I was a virgin she looked at me and called me this making my perception of myself tainted. I knew I wasn't but her words were powerful, I was never able to accept myself as I was. I had to try to please anyone who didn't appear to accept me by trying to be who *they* wanted me to be. One thing I knew about myself—I was a leader. I just couldn't get to the person I knew was in me.

When someone doesn't believe in you I've found it's only because they can't believe in who they are. I always wanted my mom to love me the way she loved my sister. She spent time with my sister, threw her birthday parties, talked with her and respected who she was. I think because my sister was born on my dad's birthday she received special treatment. It was like that was his birthday gift. I tried everything to get my mom to love me, but it never worked.

I recall a time when my mom realized a lot of my dreams had come true. She went to a voodoo doctor who told her I wouldn't live to see eighteen. My mom told me she shared some things about me to the lady, but she never said what she told her. The lady supposedly put a curse on my life. At first, I was a little afraid. I didn't understand why my own mom needed to see this woman My mom came home, flung the door open and said, "That woman said you won't live to be eighteen!" I was only sixteen then. I wondered who would want their own daughter dead. I cried for years after that because I never knew what she said and I didn't know what I could have done that my own mother needed to see this woman and accept that she said this about me. She never mentioned her reaction to what the lady told her whether she didn't want me to die or whether it even bothered her that it was said. From that I'll encourage anyone reading this book by saying to you never let people's opinions or judgements define you forget what they think even if it's a family member because that's not who God says you are.

When your mother doesn't want you, it causes a lot of emotional issues. I was sad. I couldn't find myself. I tried. I even remember when my mom told me I couldn't be a school patrol when I was seven years old; I was so hurt. Other parents allowed it, but my mom always had an excuse for why I couldn't do things.

One day I told myself, "I'm going to be a school patrol anyway." I didn't have a patrol belt, but I said, "I'm going to help cross these children." I stepped out into the street, put my arm out, and stopped the car with my hand. I was so proud of myself while those kids walked across the street. When I turned my head to see the car in front of me, my mom and dad were in the car. I was shocked. The one day I was proud of myself and did something I wanted to do, I got in trouble. My mom snatched me and said, "Get in this car." I got my behind torn up when we got home, but I was willing to risk that just to have a moment to do something I wanted.

Emotional pain can stop you in your tracks if you let it, simply because it can bind you to your past. Some people don't know how to let their past stay in the past. When you don't talk about your pain or work through it, you attract friends that are not good for you. You become close with your anger; it's your friend. You hang onto anger to fight the people who hurt you. You use your friend named "self-pity" to let you make excuses for how you feel. "Fear" tell you that you can't move forward, so you stay where you are. There's also "dépression," which is what you hold onto when you don't feel like fighting for your life. Last but not least, "hatred" mixed with "jealousy," Can be a dangerous feeling to have it has destroyed families and killed people. I have seen people hate, but when it's mixed with jealousy, it's an explosive bomb. Jealousy can cause you to hate the fact that people are doing better than you and question why your life is so bad. These bad "friends" help you find people just like you. You start attracting what's in you because you attract what you are.

God knows we can't bare all this burden and emotional hurt, so He tells us in Deuteronomy 31:8, "The Lord himself goes before you and will be with you; he will never leave you nor forsake you. Do not be afraid; do not be discouraged."

When people like my family or friends would leave me, I felt abandoned and alone. I had so many people leave me and it was hard to bear. I then read God wouldn't forsake me and I had to find out what forsake meant. When I found out, God told me, "DeeDee I won't ever abandon you or leave you alone emotionally or spiritually."

I was so filled with love, knowing someone could love me for me and not look down on me for not being what they felt I should be. God knew what gifts he had given me; he knew who I was. I was overjoyed to know that when I was at my lowest, God would be there to help me and was willing to carry my load for me. I had found a friend in Jesus.

The friends you draw to yourself start hanging around, or the relationships you keep jumping in and out of are only because you feel comfortable with someone just like you. You hang around whom you feel comfortable with, and most of the time, we say, "They understand me," right? Yet, some people won't help you confront your demons, they want you to stay in that place, the same place they are in, so they can't help you. Get around someone who will challenge you, stand up to you when you are wrong, and truly love you.

Sometimes we spend time with people, who can spot our weaknesses and use us, and we are so vulnerable, we can't see it. That's why getting into any relationship and you not whole and healthy is not wise, because you can't see while you are hurting and vulnerable, it's better to take a break away from people and get you together, love on you and let God love on you more. Then you can see clearly that love should make us better, not worse and it doesn't seek to hurt you.

You can win and rise above the pain you carry if you're willing to put down your pride and face yourself.

CHAPTER THREE

Rejection and Validation

We all hate rejection. I felt rejected first by my dad because we didn't spend enough time together. It always seemed like I had to ask to be around him. I also felt rejected by my siblings because they were so much older than me and they never invited me to hang out with them. I never knew how to deal with rejection, but I tried to accept it, and pretend it didn't bother me, but it did it controlled how I approached people and how I responded to someone who just was being honest with a no answer I always took it wrong, I went straight to negative Rejection is a hard thing to handle when you are young. I had such a dark tunnel to go through when it came to rejection, and to counteract that rejection, I needed validation. I was willing to do a lot to be validated. I compromised who I was: a kind hearted person who was passionate and full of life, and dreamed of being the best singer I could be. I loved people and was willing to help anyone who needed it, but being rejected caused me to want to hide that part of myself in fear of being told someone didn't want me.

As a kid I was called black by children in school and sometimes by some kids in church, it seemed like if you weren't light skinned something was wrong with you. Back in the 70s racism was more obvious and in our culture if you were too dark skinned you were teased. I didn't think I was pretty because I was teased for being dark-skinned. For instance, when I was with my sister, it appeared as if boys were drawn to her because she was light-skinned, at least that's what my mom told me. I grew to believe being darker-skinned was not accepted. I wondered what it would take for a boy to like me. I started to not like myself, because I based how I felt about myself on everyone else's feelings and actions toward me.

Rejection And Validation

Rejection can leave you feeling worthless. Depending on the kind of rejection, it can destroy you if you let it. Being rejected makes you feel as though people need to validate you.

I remember being fourteen years old and seeing a family member a sister of mines talking to a boy I thought I loved. He was good looking. I talked to him almost every day. I didn't know he was talking to her too; she never told me. She and I had problems between us, but I never knew it was a big deal. Later, the same boy wouldn't answer my calls. I couldn't understand why he wouldn't respond. One night, I went to the skating rink and I was so excited to hear that same boy was there, so I went looking for him. When I looked up in the balcony, there he was kissing my sister my breath left my body. I was angry. I shouted to her, "What are you doing?"

She said, "He doesn't want you."

I called my mom crying. She was so angry and she came and picked us up. While I was there, it hurt worse because he didn't even care he had hurt me. They acted like I hadn't existed.

The boy ended up telling me that he was sorry he had been talking to her too, but she was my own blood. I felt unaccepted at that point. I didn't know how to survive that. From that day on, I didn't feel good about myself because I had been abused, rejected by my own mother, and had no real relationship with my dad. I didn't even know how to get through, but I remembered the teachings I had in church about forgiveness. I fought myself every day to forgive, now I'll tell you somethings I forgave, but somethings I still held onto.

What I can tell you about validation is once you feel the need to be accepted by someone, you then base everything on how those particular people feel about you. You try to find love in almost anybody. The opposite can also be true, and you can become a cold-hearted person who blames everyone for the hurt you carry. I didn't realize that the reason I always needed someone to say nice things about me was because of my dad's opinion of me. I remember I was a good girl I had one boyfriend his name was Arthur and I loved him. My dad on the other hand felt he wasn't good enough for me of course I didn't know that until he told me that I needed an older man. I didn't want an older man and one night I heard him call me a whore to his wife I was so hurt and I cried for days in his house, and one day I just decided to move. I never told him but I held on to that and it was in my head that, that's how men thought of me. I couldn't be open to men the way I wanted to be because I felt that if my own dad feels that way what other men feel about me. I not only felt that way but I also felt that he said this behind my back, it was like a sense of betrayal to me and trust was further from my heart for people. I know that if my own dad would talk about me then who else would betray me that way. I held on to it for a long time and it ruined the way I perceived people, the way I felt about me.

Because we hold on to our resentments and accept anything that comes our way to get the attention we looking for. I say anything because some of this mess people bring to us if we would wake up we would be ashamed of what we got ourselves into. We have to spiritually wake up. For instance, when I was eighteen years old there was a guy who was nice to me. I was so excited that he paid attention to me. He was attractive and I was sure his flirting meant he was interested, but it turned out he didn't see me that way. Because I had been so hurt, it left me open to latch on to any kindness that came my way.

I never thought I would have been so vulnerable, but after being made to feel like I wasn't wanted, whether the person meant it or not, it still left a pain deep inside me. It was no one else's problem but mine. I thought to myself, *maybe I'm too black* because I was told light-skinned girls always got the boys. This kind of thinking hindered my growth as person, because I didn't feel good enough and it wasn't anyone's job to make me feel the way I was supposed to feel about me, but it became so important to me to be accepted and loved.

What I didn't realize was I didn't love myself the way I needed to. I had allowed other people's opinions to control my way of thinking about myself. I had so much to deal with when it came to me, so much I didn't like about myself, but I still wanted someone else to like and love me, so I searched for validation from people. I wanted others to praise and approve me for my looks, and my decisions, and choices in life. I needed approval because I had been told so many negative things that by time I got to my teenage years, I had no idea who I was anymore. Maybe I never knew all that was in me.

I placed my life in the hands of other people all the time because I was more concerned about how they felt about me. I did things because someone else said I should, when I was responsible for my own choices in life.

It's never what people say that makes you who you are; it's always what God says about you that make you the man or woman you are. I hated when people acted like they didn't think I was good enough. Then I realized I hated the way I didn't feel like I was good enough. I didn't know how to accept who I was because I allowed the opinions of others to control the way I thought about myself.

If you don't start accepting who you are and embracing the fact that you are not like everyone else, you can't expect people to truly accept you. People treat you the way you treat yourself. Most of the times the people you trying to get to accept you are hurt too, some were traumatize themselves, and need to be loved. We don't see it at the time but later when you grow up on the inside as a person in spirit and mind you mature enough to see you are not so bad they could never have accepted you because they had issues themselves.

I knew I couldn't measure up to other people's standards, but I tried every day, even when those same people didn't measure up to their own standards. For instance, I remember I was very easily hurt when people would talk about me. I had to grow to realize that I couldn't control what people had to say, but I was expected to overcome what they said. I had to be strong. I knew I hadn't grown to that point, but they needed to grow in that area too because when someone would say something about them they would be affected by it. I realized that some people only give you advice but it doesn't mean they live by what they say.

I know it's not easy, but if you are trying hard to fit into someone else's way of doing things to please them, you will be miserable, because you can never measure up. You can only be the best you.

I tried to fit in with my family, tried to find my place in school, tried to be accepted as a woman, tried to look like everyone else, tried to get people to like and accept me, and tried to feel accepted in my personal relationships with men. I don't care how you do it; truthfully, your validation can never come from people. I realized that because I was so needy for love from someone else it was draining to the other person. I didn't have love for myself so no amount of love from another person was enough. We have to love ourselves enough to give love to other people. Then I also acknowledged that I didn't need validation from man because God had already accepted and qualified me. Man can never give you the same acceptance as God. The way we feel about ourselves can determine the outcome of our lives. You may have to go through many things before you get it. I did; I went through so much hurt and disappointment before I got it in my heart that no one can love me the way God does. My biggest problem was feeling sorry for myself all the time. I felt life wasn't fair to me because of my abuse, I hated my life sometimes, that divorce really tore our family apart and I don't think we all really recovered from it . I didn't see anything positive, I felt only negative was happening in my life. I also realized that I didn't like my mom because of the hurt that I felt instead of love. I also felt misunderstood by my siblings because I didn't believe it was possible that they could relate to my pain or my rejection when it appeared they were getting what they needed from our parents. I starved for hugs and encouragement from anywhere I could get it because my self-esteem was so low. In my experience, people with God-given love, filled with the Holy Ghost, will love you the way God does. You will get that comfort from Him through them. Don't think only God gives love, because He can show it through people too.

I have a friend I met in Texas who told me, "Deedee you don't need validation from anyone." I thank her today for that because it's true. Only God can heal you and pick you up. He'll give you that confidence you need to do the things you need to do to be the man or woman of God you need to be.

Now, when I am around someone who makes me feel I have to question myself, I pray about that relationship because I know God will put me around people who will build me up and keep me encouraged, not make me feel like I have to question who I am. I suggest associating yourself with positive people who only have your best interests in mind.

I remember when I went to church, I was so messed up. I was emotionally damaged from the gossip, and the favoritism, and the jealousy in another church so when I got there, I needed help and healing. Everyone was nice, but people are always going to be people. Eventually, I got to know some people, but then I wanted to fit in the cliques. I wanted validation and I didn't know God had to get the praise. Sometimes I just kept to myself because I had no confidence.

When people start praising you, you want more praise, especially when you have never had it.

I got high off of that the feeling of being accepted by people. Then, one day, it all stopped. The opposite started to happen. I was being talked about and criticized. People would say things like, "She needs to dress better," and "maybe she should just be quiet." I couldn't understand what I had done to deserve that. I tried everything to get people in the church to change their minds about me. I tried to talk to them and reason with them, but I ended up making it worse. At the time I wasn't strong enough to take the criticism. Some of them didn't even want to be bothered with me. I was crushed in the church. I couldn't blame anyone, but I didn't know that at that time. I only knew I had to do something different.

It took me years to figure it all out—the way I felt about myself caused others to treat me as such. I was on the pity party bus. It drove me all around, but people knew I wanted the attention. They knew I wanted validation and acceptance. Some of them refused to give it to me. I was eager to be like everyone else—loved.

I was all over the place for years. My mind stayed focused on wanting other people to see me as a good person who could be liked. I realized later that I had a bad attitude and all the hurt that I have been through affected my thoughts. I let how other people viewed me cloud my thoughts on how I saw myself. I then decided it wasn't as important to be what everyone else was; it was more important to be whom I was, and then my journey started. I decided it was time for me to get to know myself so I could begin to focus on what was more important.

I saw it was my responsibility to fix my life, to line my thinking up with the Bible and not blame anyone for all of the things that happened to me. I had to take what I went through and do something with it rather than sit in self-pity and do nothing with my life. I needed to accept myself and use my mess as a message for other people. It was all up to me. So I say to you that you don't need validation from anyone; it's up to you to change your situation and make a difference.

Chapter Four

Stuffing the Pain

We have so many people who stuff their feelings in the world today. I know people say, "Let's just drop it," and we say, "I'm over that." Of course we say that, but truthfully most of us stuff our emotions because we really don't want to deal with them.

Throughout my life, I was a stuffer too. I didn't think I was because I had always been open with my feelings. Looking back, I realized I was a stuffer because I wouldn't forgive. When you're a stuffer you don't want to deal with anything; it's easy to walk away or run from situations. Most people have a hard time dealing with life itself; it's such a challenge to them that it causes them to shut down and give up.

When you have problems and don't want to talk about or deal with them, you'll eventually explode like a bomb. Not dealing with your problems only hurts you, no one else, because it allows you to live in a falsehood that does not exist.

Most people live in denial of what this does to us as people. When we put things off and don't face them, it only leaves us in a state of not being able to forgive. How do we go on with life when we leave things we haven't dealt with in our lives? How do we function when problems come and we won't address them?

I've seen people in pain who have this issue and if you say one more thing to them, they will explode. I watched this behavior all my life, in the church and in my home; I can say I became this person in my life at one time. I ran away from problems and avoided anyone who tried talk about it. I walked around smiling, hoping no one would ask me what was wrong with me, because I wasn't ready to deal with the issues I carried within myself. I thought pushing it down and moving on would fix it. I was just stuffing my emotions, putting them inside, and said, "I'm fine. It's not bothering me. I'm over it." At least, that what I thought until someone I loved left me and reminded me of that situation. Stuffing is what we do as people because it's an easy problem-solver if you good at it.

Sometimes, if a situation is too painful to face or deal with, we feel better walking away and saying, "I'm over it." We don't feel it's necessary to even open that can of worms, but truthfully if we don't open the can; it sits in our house and takes up space. Just like that can of worms you have in your heart, unopened and brewing inside.

I know I had a can of worms sitting in my spiritual house—that problem or situation that was too painful to talk about. I couldn't see myself even being vulnerable to someone to open up about it; I was simply too embarrassed to even say what it was. I thought if I would leave it with God, it was done, and sometimes, that's okay. However, our testimony isn't ours, its God's.

When God delivers you from something, you have to tell it. It belongs to Him; He wants the glory.

I thought because I went to church, I didn't have to talk about it. We were taught to just give it to Jesus. That's true, but the Bible tells us to cast our cares upon Him because He cares for us, and that's what I did. I then realized I was using that command not to talk about something that I was too embarrassed to say. I found ways to keep it while not dealing with it as long as I could, which is not casting it, especially if you know you need to face it and deal with the pain of it. I know you are saying, "Some things God has to fix." It's true; some things you do leave in God's hands, but you have to fully turn it over to Him in order for Him to work it out.

Some people hold onto pain because they don't know how to let it go. Their pain is truly their weapon. Let's take anger as an example. When you are in pain and walking around with it, you feel like it's been there so long, it's a part of you and you may not pay attention to your behavior. Let's go through this one together. Someone made you mad and you didn't show it at first, then something else happened after that and you let it build up because that situation got to you. They hurt your feelings. Because you didn't deal with the first incident, the bottle containing your feelings was shaken and when the top came off, you exploded.

We are that bottle when we are angry and hold on to pain. That pain is our own; we own it the moment we allow it to sit and fester in our hearts. We try to put it on others and say they made us mad or angry, or think, *if they hadn't done this I wouldn't be angry*, but the truth is, we had the anger sitting inside and all someone had to do was shake us up a little and it spilled out.

Anger comes from a dark place in us. I know we all get angry sometimes, but this anger I'm talking about is not a good anger it's when you get emotionally out of control.. I'm talking about the anger that you had since your childhood that became your weapon to use if someone crossed you the wrong way. Normally stuffers become angry, cold, and self-absorbed. When you start stuffing, it changes your attitude and the way you treat people. It makes you shut down and feel isolated.

No one likes feeling alone. Most of the time, we become untrusting and we don't allow ourselves to become vulnerable. Looking back, I see my life as I hid and stuffed things when I couldn't bare the truth and embarrassment. I know how it feels to put away the things that hurt. I stuffed because I didn't trust anyone to tell my hurt to. I was so hurt and my pain led me to make bad decisions in my life. I know when a person is in pain and can't express it, they smile all the time to hide their feelings But our eyes are the windows to our soul and you can see the pain in their eyes even though they are smiling yet they go home or even in their car and cry. Sometimes, the pain pushed me into an emotional state where I made decisions off of how I felt instead of waiting until I calmed down and could think. For instance, I remember a situation when me and my ex-husband got into a heated argument, and I felt betrayed by the way he embarrassed me before my family. I quickly wanted a divorce. I know I was upset and not in any condition to make a decision that was good for me.

When you are angry, all you need is for someone to say one more thing to you and they will be punished for everything that everyone did to you that day.

We are not here to handle everything alone. We are here with each other and the God of all told us in 1 Thessalonians 5:11, "Therefore encourage one another and build each other up, just as in fact you are doing." We are responsible for each other and we have the ability to keep each other lifted and covered daily.

There's no reason we should want to handle anything alone. We have each other for council so we can make sure we are making the right choices.

I pray before I make decisions, but I also use the tools God gave me to be able to connect with Him. The scripture says, in Matthew 18:20, "For where two or three gather in my name, there am I with them."

When we realize that, as long as we pretend to be okay and not reach out to each other and confess our faults, we are not obeying the Word.

I know people who tell me I always dealt with things by myself and that I'm not used to reaching out to others for help. It's understandable because I have to be willing to trust and be open. I believe that the real reason we don't reach out is because we have issues with trust.

These issues get in the way of our decisions to be able to humble ourselves and drop our pride to get the help we need. Sometimes, our distrust comes from how we treat others and we think we can't trust others because of what they have done. In reality, we can't trust because of what we've done to others.

We tend to be more afraid of what others may do to us because we know how we are. It's like a man or woman who cheats—they always accuse the spouse or the significant other of cheating because they believe what they are doing will be done to them, so they don't trust the other person, but they truly don't trust themselves.

When you don't trust yourself, you can't trust anyone because you think people are going to do to you what you have done to other people, and you can't trust the flesh anyway. Let me tell you God never told you to trust flesh he said trust in God. Trust the God in that person, and you may say what if they don't have God well you have to trust the God in you. You start living in fear that you're going to get back what you dished out. Karma is something no one can dodge; it shows up whether you want it to or not.

When you are talking to someone and anger is your drive, if you are trying to get a point across, it won't reach them because all they will hear is your anger and how you said it to them. They won't hear what you're saying; they will only hear how you say it. So if they needed help at the moment from you, you failed because you allowed your carnal behavior to get in the way of the Lord, who may have needed to use you to help that person receive their deliverance.

I always use this example to help people understand that, you are a servant and your behavior affects your service. You can't serve people and in your heart you're feeling another way toward them an ungodly way that would get in the way of your service. For instance, if you made a big dinner and you put all your work into it and felt proud of what you had done. All your guests show up and sit at the table, waiting to eat what you prepared. You serve the food, slamming it down on plates, throwing the plates down, all as part of your serving. You appear mad about giving the food to them, so how can they enjoy the food if you are serving it with anger or an attitude? You defeated your own purpose of even having the dinner if you're not doing it in love.

It's the same when you serve people with the gifts you have; if you don't make sure your heart is pure and clean before you go to them, you won't do it in love because the whole purpose of serving is to be motivated by love. It doesn't matter whether they are a Christian or not; you want to make sure your love walk is in order so someone is encouraged by you or saved.

The danger of a stuffer is their silence. Their silence is another way of saying, "Leave me alone." It becomes isolation which is not good for anyone. It is also emotional abuse, and when women or men do this it's a way of punishing your mate or person you in a relationship with. I watched my own dad do it to my mother and I also have experience from being in relationships with people man or woman so messed up on the inside they declare this is the way. Let me advise you it's only the way out the door of a relationship. When you isolate yourself, especially as a Christian, you allow the enemy to keep you away from relationships. I'm sorry to say some people are in relationships but do not have a real relationship because of the isolation between them and their partner. When you are in a relationship and cannot be open and relate, there is a major problem that you are not admitting. You can't be in a true relationship without talking and if you are not talking, you need to find out why.

Unfortunately, stuffing makes you not talk. You are so bound down with things that you feel are overwhelming that you don't know the first place to start. I remember when I was going through a bad time in my first marriage. I was so overwhelmed with taking care of the kids, paying the bills, and trying to be there for my husband, it felt like it all hit me at one time. I decided to keep it to myself out of pure embarrassment. My sister would ask how I was doing but I had to keep it together and be an example, at least that's the way I was taught, but truthfully I was suffering from emotional and mental abuse. I know at that time he was not trying to do this or maybe it was all he knew at that time, but the abuse was very damaging to me. It was hard to be treated with manipulation and game playing with your mind all the time. I believe half of this behavior he learned was truthfully taught to him. It affected me so, that my son thought he would have to admit me into a mental institution. I was literally losing my mind, I did not tell anyone because the church world lifted him in a certain place and I was nothing in their sight. Who would believe me this caused me to hide and not reveal the hurt that came with it. I had no one to cry out to I was scared to say anything to anyone, because backbiting was real in the church. We could have gotten help if we both knew who to go to whom to trust, I believe it could have turned around and I could have made better decisions. Not talking caused more emotional problems for me, because keeping it all in destroyed me. When you don't talk and you are married, it shows the lack of being able to handle some situations. Whether you are married or dating, you have to be open to be able to develop something more fulfilling. Marriage is the institution of God and many people don't take it serious, it is not man made but God ordained it. I have to say that because I was already abused in my earlier life it just caused more traumas to me emotionally. I realized that we did not know how to be married to each other and without that knowledge we failed at it.

We miss this experience not willing to trust ourselves to someone else. First we don't trust ourselves to God so then if we don't trust God, we will never be able to fully know how to trust others.

You will always think *I'll just trust myself,* but even *you* will let yourself down. I know "doing you" will only cheat yourself out of good healthy relationships, whether it's marriage, family, or friendship. The major reasons why relationships fail are because we don't know how to have them, we don't know what we are doing, and we also don't know how to pick a mate. Lack of knowing, now I say lack of knowledge the key things God says we should have in any relationship we will fail without the know how to be married or to be in a healthy friendship. You have to know what you are doing and how to treat someone, and you can't do it without the Agape Love because it's unconditional and you need it to love people. Love is a choice not a feeling.

I understand why we don't talk sometimes. I even understand the times that we are in where there is almost no way you can trust people like we use to, so we need to be better examples and have better character so that someone can see the God in us and get the help they need but always remember we have God to look to and we don't have to carry any burden by ourselves. We can't do it on our own if we do it leads to destruction. We are not designed to handle things on our own. God made us so we have each other to help us bare one another's burdens.

I also say this because suicide is on the rise and most people who don't express their emotions think of just giving up on life, committing suicide seems to be their only option. If I'm talking to you, you are not alone and you don't have to feel like no one cares because God does and He has people who do also. It's the enemy's job to make you feel isolated and to destroy your mental health. Remember, your mind is a powerful thing, and before you allow the devil to put bad thoughts about you and who you are in your mind, I encourage you to talk to someone and let them fight with you and pray with you. We are in this together and no one is without pain in life, so please never feel like you are alone and no one understands.

The other danger is sickness. Most people who don't talk about their problems end up stressed and sick. Within themselves, they feel like they're okay, but walking around with anger, hatred, or any other bad feeling hurts you inside. It allows you to get depressed and speak negatively because what's in you has to come out.

We put our masks on and say we're okay, but we are dying inside. Using a mask to cover pain only hurts us; it never resolves anything. Some people die alone because they didn't talk to anyone. People may be on social media, but in reality, their story isn't the one that they are sharing. They are in pain.

We hide behind anything we can to cover our pain: we drink, smoke, have multiple sexual partners—anything but admit, "I'm hurting." With all of that, it makes us sick emotionally and physically. That's why God wants us to cast our cares on Him, because we weren't made for that type of stress. Remember when you don't love you, you go to these things, and if you don't love you, you can't truly love someone else. I say you deceiving yourself and that person.

Stuffing does not have a good effect on your life. So try finding someone you know can pray and get in touch with God. Do not gossip, but know how to keep a friend's problem and go to God with it. That's the kind of person you can trust, because pretending you are okay is never good, as you only deceive yourself in the end. Try crying out to God about your problems and opening up to Him. He will help you see yourself as He created you and help you change.

Chapter Five

The Pain of Addictions

I believe addictions are one of the strongest demons to fight. It doesn't matter what addictions you have, when it's a bad addiction, it's a fight to let it go. However, there is a good addiction and that's being addicted to the Word of God. The addictions I will name that I am familiar with are there to destroy you. I am a witness to this because I had two addictions that I've had to battle.

My first addiction was food. I didn't know I was addicted. I ate when I felt like it. I was a feeling eater. If I felt sad, I ate. If I felt good, I ate. If I was depressed, I ate. I ate out of my emotions for years. I started after having kids and my self-esteem went down when I gained weight from each pregnancy. I didn't know how to express myself, I was always told to be quiet, I never felt like the people who were close to me valued my opinion and when I talked about my weight issues, but I was so concerned about how others felt about me that I couldn't see what I felt of myself.

I remember comparing myself to others all the time and when I looked at myself, I didn't feel beautiful. It was hard to look myself in the mirror because I didn't want to be fat; I wanted to be beautiful and in shape. I didn't want to look the way I did.

Well, I got pregnant again. My two oldest sons are one year apart, and being a new mom it was very difficult to take care of them and make sure I was caring for myself. I didn't plan to have them so close together. I became depressed and wondered whether I would be a good mother. Then, we were in church and women all around me seemed to have themselves together, and I felt left out. When I went home, I would eat and not think anything of it until I gained more weight. Don't get me wrong, I wasn't two hundred pounds, but I was bigger than usual. I thought maybe it was just baby fat and I'd be all right.

A year and a half later, I got pregnant again, and then I really ate. I ate so much; I would eat even when I was full. I knew it was a problem, so I lost weight and was proud of myself, and then I got pregnant again. By that time my starting weight was more than I wanted to be. I knew I had a problem that was more than "I had children."

I had issues in my marriage. I had to face the problems I had and how I felt. I ate instead of dealing with the problems around me. I remember it got so bad because my husband at the time had never been in a relationship before, so he wasn't aware of the things he was doing that triggered my scars from the past. He was unemotional, and I didn't realize that it was hurting me. I also didn't realize he couldn't give me what he didn't have, which was the love I should have had for myself. I was told to just let go of the past by the elders of the church. It was the right thing to do, but some people have deep issues that don't go away by saying, "I let it go," so they need counseling.

I know my eating was a big problem and I became obese. Sometimes I couldn't talk to anyone because I didn't want to be judged, so I ate. I didn't want to be looked down on and I also put a lot of pressure on myself to measure up to others.

I loved birthday cake, so every time I had a chance to eat it, I would. It didn't matter how many pieces I ate; it made me feel better.

Overeating is a sin. Philippians 3:19 says, "Their destiny is destruction, their god is their stomach, and their glory is in their shame. Their mind is set on earthly things."

There are additional Scriptures about overeating, but that one stuck out the most.

I remember when I was down on a particular day; I didn't know how to come out of it. I recall that day my husband had brought a birthday cake home and he knew I loved it, so he let me know he brought it home for me. I decided to eat the cake the next day. This may sound simple, but it was not because I wouldn't just eat one piece. I would overeat and not care. That day was no different. I decided to get away from the children and go in the bathroom and eat. That is where God delivered me from my eating addiction. As I sat with my mouth watering, about to go at it, the Lord spoke to me. He asked me, "What are you doing? You do not trust me. You're going to the cake with your problems instead of coming to me."

I knew I was wrong and I repented. I was overwhelmed and wanted to make my flesh feel good, but my spirit suffered. We all have things we put before God and use to get away as an escape, but that's making those things into a god and God is a jealous God.

That wasn't my only addiction. I also became a workaholic, my second addiction. I worked almost a full day. I would work eighteen hours a day; it was the drive I had. I thought *you're doing something, girl*. Well, I wasn't. My family was falling apart. My kids were raising themselves. My house wasn't clean the way I wanted it. My personal life was a mess. I caught myself getting away from everything and working was my means of getting

The Pain Of Addictions

away. I would get a high off of working. I didn't want to go home; I just had to work.

I didn't realize it until I got hurt on the job. We were remodeling the store and one of the employees pulled part of the gondola apart and the steel part of it hit my foot. At first I thought I was okay until my foot swelled up and I could hardly walk. I eventually went to the emergency room and then to the workman's compensation doctor. He took me off the job because my foot collapsed due to torn ligaments. I made that job my god. I was so afraid when I found out the extent of my injury because I had to get surgery to repair it. The procedure was called reconstruction of the foot. I didn't want surgery but I had no other choice; my bone was sticking out of my foot due to the injury. God spoke to me before I surgery and said, "This job didn't take care of you. I did, and I'm going to show you."

Well, He did because when I got hurt, God showed me in a dream He was going to give me ten thousand dollars. He blessed me the next year with that money and showed me that He supplies my needs. I realized even though I treated God like I took care of myself God had mercy on me and allowed me to get to get my finances right.

Sometimes, we have so much pain in our lives; we don't know where to start to clean out our baggage. We walk around with a bag and think that no one sees us, but we are wrong. People see you; they may not all understand, but some people see you because they are carrying the same bag you are.

Walking around with this pain is like carrying a luggage bag that you haven't unpacked. You forgot to unload it or maybe you're just too lazy to unpack. We've all been there; we get back from a vacation and don't feel like unpacking, so we just put the suitcase in the closet and let it sit. We forget that the bag is there; sometimes we get so busy that we think we'll come back to it but we are overshadowed with what's going on in our lives. That's how it is with any addiction: life hits and then we start thinking about the past, that bag we forgot we hid in the closet is what we bring back into our lives—the dirty stuff we never cleaned.

When we carry that dirty stuff around in our hearts, we are like that baggage that we forgot to unpack. A house with things cluttered and thrown in closets, not in order is an example of how we may feel on the inside. Sometimes closets are full of things from the past that we hold onto. Our hearts is one of the most important part of the body God wants. He said in Mark 12:30 Love the Lord your God with all your heart and with all your soul and with all your mind and with all your strength. I look at this scripture and wonder do we have room for God because if you have to love him with all your heart, then with all the things in our heart where is the room to love him with all. We first have to empty out our heart to God to give him our all. I believe we so use to giving it to people and things because we can see that, that we don't know how to give him our everything. We have nothing to give if we already gave it away to a drug, a person or a idle we have to be careful that we don't give our heart to something that can't help us and make us better people, I say it so easy to do.

I am one of those people. I had a major problem with letting go of things and clothes that I couldn't wear anymore; holding on to the past and my closet was all out of order. I decided to tackle the situation by first getting rid of the clothes I couldn't wear anymore. I had to accept that I had gained weight, so I could deal with whatever I was holding on to. By accepting I ate my way to my weight I also had to love me where I was, because I knew as long as I hated myself for being bigger I would never lose my weight. I also knew that in order for new things to come in my life I had to let go of the old, so I finally let things go. It's the same with your insides and emotions: you have things that you hold onto from the past and if you don't let them go, they cause you to be weighed down and depressed. Don't allow your heart to be like that cluttered closet. You have to decide to get rid of the past.

Addiction is an escape from the pain we refuse to deal with. Some of us can't face ourselves; seeing the truth is often the biggest problem. So we tend to run from ourselves, but blame others as we go, because facing ourselves would mean we would have to change and that's something an addict finds hard to do. Some addictions are more harmful than others, but they all take away from God, and even though we know this, we still tend to go to something to help us instead of trusting God.

There are many people who feel they have the answer to this problem. I have seen people transfer addictions, thinking they can trade one addiction for another. It doesn't work that way though.

You can't get the true help you need without God. He is the only one who knows how to get you out of your mess. He made us and He knows us. Psalm 139:1-3 says, "You have searched me, Lord, and you know me, you know when I sit and when I rise, you perceive my thoughts from afar, you discern my going out and my lying down; you are familiar with all my ways." God knows everything that we are going through and with Him, you can conquer anything, but without Him, you are nothing.

We also need honesty. We have to be willing to be honest with ourselves. I think most addictions come from having too many secrets. We can't overcome anything in our lives by hiding. Hiding is the most popular thing an addict does. We don't want anyone to know who we are inside. Hiding sometimes consists of not being able to face yourself. Yet, being honest with yourself and God will always help you break the addiction.

Sometimes the fear of judgment from people can make you hide. Sometimes to admit you have an addiction is another reason to hide. We as people can have a hard time revealing our true selves and accepting who we are.

Talking is the last piece we need to find healing. I think most people who struggle with addiction don't talk. Isolation is what feels better because they dwell on what they want to do and don't want to be talked out of it.

The enemy always wants you to shut down and not talk. Talking allows you to make sense of what you are feeling and make good decisions. When you are fighting an addiction, you have to be open and talk about your feelings every time you are disappointed or hurt.

These three things are important because it helps you be sober-minded and practice self-control. Addictions are hard when pain is the driving force. When you don't deal with the reason behind it, it will control and destroy your life. You will lose everything behind the addiction. It takes over your thought process and sometimes kills your relationships.

Some people never recover from the addiction because they lose everything in the process and this is the key to this problem. If you don't deal with the pain, it only takes you to a place from where you may never come back.

Depending on the addiction, some addictions can kill you, such as substance abuse, sexual abuse, or eating disorders. These addictions, amongst others I have not named, will destroy you.

The addiction people most talk about is drugs. Most drug addictions are deadly and hurtful to go through with the person. The family suffers just as much as the person with addiction.

There are other addictions such as shopping, which can also bring hardship to a marriage due to a financial burden. Most people, of course, choose this road to go down but the addictions are used to replace the pain that they refuse to cope with or face.

Let's take sexual addiction as an example. If this is a person's way of coping, they go from person to person trying to get a feeling from the sexual act. It's like a high; once you use it to numb you; you want it all the time. Sex is used the same way and behind it is a pain you wouldn't know happened to the person. I've been in a relationship where my partner was addicted to pornography, and it was tough to deal with. I didn't know that my partner had a problem until I found the material; I felt betrayed. At the time he wouldn't admit his problem because of his shame. Most of the time someone won't tell you, either because they are embarrassed or are too caught up and don't want to stop. Someone may think it will fulfill their sexual desires. Sometimes a person chooses not to reveal what's going on. It hurts them more than it hurts you, because they lose everything to these addictions. For people who have been molested or raped, opening up is frightening to them.

When it comes to revealing your pain, someone would have to be able to handle you the way God says, not in judgment. Scripture tells us in Galatians 6:1,

"Brothers and sisters, if someone is caught in a sin, you who live by the Spirit should restore that person gently. But watch yourselves, or you also may be tempted." It's important we don't sit in God's seat and judge His servants because we aren't in the wrong at the moment. I believe when Paul addressed us about this matter, he was concerned about the love and compassion we have for one another. Addiction—like any other sin—is to be handled according to the Word of God. We have to understand the person's problems and put ourselves in their shoes. We have to have empathy and consider that we can fall at any moment as well. It may not be *that* sin, but we can be overtaken by sin and be ashamed because of the way we handled a situation.

It is important to understand God is concerned about how we treat each other, so don't be quick to say what a person should do until you have walked in their shoes. You don't know the trauma most people have been through that has put them in a particular situation.

I believe most people don't talk about the pain families go through when they deal with the addiction of the loved ones. I know because my husband had an addiction that we lived with every day, it almost destroyed our marriage. I was feeling helpless and angry it took God to help me get through the hurt. Both my husband and I decided to go to meetings and complete the twelve-step program and now we are stable. My program is Al anon. It is a great program for families, and I definitely recommend it. My children had also felt abandoned and lived in fear along with me. They were able to talk to someone about their pain, which was also helpful. I am here to tell you that you have to trust God and do not try to control the person or change them; it only hurts the situation. The saying, "Let go and let God," is also true. It is not an easy task and there is pain behind it. When people are hurt, they hurt others. If you are hurt and holding onto pain, whether you forgive others or forgive yourself, you have to let go of the pain in order to be able to love. As long as you ignore your pain, you will kill any relationship you are in because someone will pay for the pain you carry. Pain is like cancer and it will eat away at you.

Some people want to save their loved ones, but sometimes they have to save themselves. Make sure you are healed first. Sometimes you may have to heal without a loved one, but don't be angry. Always have grace and don't be manipulated by them; just be wise. It's okay to love someone, but you can help them see themselves better by getting yourself together by changing you and not walking in anger or bitterness.

When people hurt you, it takes God to help you forgive, and you have to be open to forgive—not for them but for you. Otherwise, you live in regret and will never learn the lesson from the situation.

We all have lessons to learn from decisions we make, whether they are good or bad decisions, we have lessons and teaching moments. We don't want to miss the moment that will make us the person God want us to be in the end.

Chapter Six

Broken Relationships

We all have experienced broken relationships in some way. Broken relationships contribute to the pains many of us carry. Sometimes we tend to hold onto relationships whether it's out of regret of how we treated that person, not knowing how we can fix or perhaps having closure from the relationship just needing them to apologize and not just forgiving them even if they never say they're sorry

My first broken relationship was with my parents. I didn't have a good example of how healthy relationships were supposed to look because I didn't have one with either of my parents. As I begin to grow, I didn't know this but I was already taught about abandonment and emotional abuse when my mom was not able to show any emotions to me. I felt alone and abandoned. I also saw abuse around me from watching my mom and dad fight all the time, and how he would beat her, I remember when my mom tried to get his attention and he didn't want to talk how she got a knife walked outside and tried to kill herself then I knew she was broken and their relationship would never be the same. We all screamed and cried it was traumatizing. My mother was never the same and neither was I. We had our good and bad days, but my bad days felt like they outweighed the good during my childhood.

I clung to my pain in broken relationships. I didn't know how to let go of the hurt and forgive. I used my pain as protection, and I felt no one would be able to hurt me. I never considered I may have hurt myself in the process. I also never considered that by holding onto the pain, I would damage other relationships.

Growing up, I always tried to get my parents' attention by singing in the church or trying to get good grades, so I could be praised like my siblings. Sometimes, I made decisions like skipping school, trying to fit in at school, but that didn't work out for me. I got caught by a teacher who really loved me.

Sometimes, our first heartbreak comes from our parents because that's where we learn who we are and how we are supposed to be. We become disappointed and begin to hold what our parents did to us against everyone. Parents, including myself, do the best they know how. But in reality, we know sometimes getting past that abandonment is the hardest thing to do. Disappointment or resentment from our parents often creates a barrier in our hearts where no one can get in. We lose trust from that first relationship and then no one can gain our trust, because we become numb and we close our hearts up where no one can get in.

Some carry their pain into other relationships. The pain is not always from relationships with parents, however; it can also be a sibling or other relative who causes pain. I know my abandonment issues also came from my older sister cutting me out her life without any explanation. We had a close relationship but because of the pain in our family, the favoritism our parents displayed created a wedge; which caused us to grow apart and not trust each other. I tried to replace her with other friends whom I called sisters but they couldn't help me through that pain and lack of forgiveness I had toward my sister at that time. It wasn't my friends' fault they couldn't bear that with me. I couldn't play the victim, because everyone has their own problems they are battling. Sometimes we give people the hurt we need to give God, who is the only one who can handle it.

Now those of you who are in a relationship and have trust issues I want to tell you that you haven't allowed yourself to be open for someone to love you. You have to trust that person is not out to hurt you. In order to do that, you have to have had emotional healing from any broken relationship that you have not dealt with and come to peace with how it ended.

It's important to understand every relationship is not intended to be long-lasting. We meet people and right away jump into relationships, without knowing if these people are supposed to be in our lives for a long time.

I have done that with not only men, but women too. I would meet a man and next thing you know we were in a relationship based off of what he said to me to make me feel wanted. Also, when it came to female friends, I would say I got a friend because she wanted to be around me. I was so happy to have someone show me some attention. I was fearful of getting hurt, though, and I was on guard all the time. I always worried about what someone thought of me.

Relationships are not supposed to help us become resentful, irritated, harsh, and angry. However, broken relationships help us learn and appreciate the experience whether we fall into a trap or it just happened to us. Don't let the enemy deceive you, telling you to hold onto resentment or regret. Every situation you experienced is there to better you, not make you worse. It takes God to help us through, and if you don't ask Him to help you, you will remain in an angry state. After a relationship has become broken, ask God to make you whole again.

We all have to admit some relationships we get into are our own fault. We, as people, all want to be loved, but when we are in pain, we are vulnerable. Some people are smart enough to see us in need of attention or love and will take advantage of it. We are responsible for that because the pain can cloud judgments.

I'm a living witness that pain can cloud judgment. I was always told by my spiritual mother, not to make any decisions based on my emotions. Yet, when we experience broken relationships, sometimes we get lonely and our motives can be based off of fear of being alone. I used to think; *maybe I'll never be in another relationship*. Those thoughts were with me a lot because of the way I felt about myself, remember relationships whether married or not especially a marriage needs to be put much thought process into, because it can distract you from God or bring you closer. You want to be in a relationship that pushes you to God and your destiny.

Sometimes, when a person leaves us, we tend to blame ourselves and think *there's something wrong with me*. It can create a feeling of abandonment and make us hold onto people we need to let go.

When a person wants to leave, let them. It only hurts you in the end, because you can't move on and take what you learned from the relationship and grow from it. Insecurity makes us react this way.

When you have emotional insecurity, it comes from some kind of fear, anxiety, or experience you had as a child. Some people carry this throughout their lives and never deal with it. Deal with what is in your past, face your pain. Whatever it is that holds you back, don't let it weigh you down and hinder your relationships in the future.

CHAPTER SEVEN

Just Deal with It

It's never easy to tell someone to "Just deal with it." It has been a real challenge in my lifetime to say this to people I love. I never want to come off as thinking their pain is not a big deal, but we have to deal with pain to grow. I have seen so many people run from pain and they run from themselves. I've asked people, "Why are you running?"

You can't run from yourself because you carry yourself everywhere you go. I remember how I ran from my own problems by not addressing them. I didn't do myself any justice by allowing pain to eat away at me day and night.

There were times I didn't want to deal with anything. I knew I had to handle my issues at some point, but it hurt too bad to even talk about them. I didn't want talk about how I was going to deal with my children's feelings about divorcing their dad, but I had to face them and how they felt. It was hard and embarrassing because I had to open up in front of my kids. I cried and told them how sorry I was that the divorce affected them the way it did. Divorce caused a lot of rebellion in my children. It was our responsibility as their parents to help them through that pain. My now ex-husband and I talked about it a lot, and we still talk to each other and have a friendship, to help them heal. I will tell you divorce is the worst death; it feels like you never really heal, but only a God can help you forgive yourself and move on after divorce.

The biggest pain I had to deal with was with my child I had with another man outside of marriage. I was so embarrassed because I didn't consider the consequences at the time and I didn't believe in having children without marriage. I was so damaged from the breakup that I didn't see that everyone would suffer from my decisions even though it happened after my divorce. I was so concerned about how people would look at me, the judgment that would come from the church world, I avoided people I should have talked to instead I ran from them but because of my pain I felt from the divorce, I made a decision to have her even though I was shamed and felt condemned because I hadn't lived the way I was called to by God. I allowed my emotions to control my decisions, but I eventually realized God still loved me even though I had let Him down. It wasn't the people who I needed to concern with; it was me I had to deal with. I had became a very impatient person, I mean I needed God to be my microwave just fix this stuff now. I was always asking him to fix something, fix my marriage, fix my children, fix my finances, fix my boss, but I realized God was using these situations to fix me. I had a hard time going through my process, but I had to face myself every day because I let myself down. God let me know He had forgiven me through listening to a testimony from gospel singer, Donnie McClurkin. Yet, I still had to forgive myself.

It was then I recognized in the midst of pain, we can make bad decisions if we don't get help and talk about what's hurting us. If we don't, it may cost us, it's always wise to seek spiritual counsel..

I don't regret my daughter; she's my blessing, and I'm grateful to God that we made it through a really rough pregnancy.

You may be avoiding certain things in your life. You may say, "You don't understand; it's too painful," but I do understand. I have so much experience when it comes to not dealing with issues as they arise. Putting healing off is never good because you avoid the root problem. When it's time to talk and be honest with you and others don't hide; we all have something to confess, we have to do just that.

I had to tell my children when they got themselves in a mess, "Don't try to avoid the mess you just made; you're only making the situation worse."

You can't keep ignoring what's in you, so you have to open up your heart and be willing to accept who you are and where you are right now.

I used to hear all the time, "You make your bed, you lay in it." I wanted my kids to stop blaming other people when they needed to take responsibility for their own actions. I teach my children that avoiding their own problems is only hurting them. It gives them a way out of accepting they have a problem. Then it allows you to blame others and not face the fact that you are responsible for your own life decisions. The lack of knowledge is what gets you to stay where you are. If you don't get knowledge life will pass you by and you will be stuck in the same situation ten years from now, because you can't stop change. I promise change happens even if you have something to do with it or not. In other words, you will change the question is what kind of change will you do. Will you change for the better or for the worse? I heard people say "Oh they'll never change", yes we all change but it's the type of change we need to be concerned about.

Have you ever noticed when you have not dealt with pain, it changes your outlook on life and how you deal with things? Most of the time, you respond to situations with your emotions. Pain brings on all kinds of emotions, especially the negative ones. Anger, wrath, jealousy, envy, strife, hatred, gluttony, selfishness—if you are battling any of these negative feelings, I challenge you to face them and be willing to submit to God for help. Stand up and challenge yourself to be better. When you are willing to accept responsibility, it can change who you are.

No one can make you change; that is up to you. Being willing to change is your new beginning. If you don't change, you're not living. The challenges we face daily should bring out the best in us and allow us to change for the better.

If this is not happening for you, I need you to challenge yourself and find where your pain begins and push through that pain to get to your next level. The Bible says in Luke 9:23 "Take up your cross and follow me." We don't always know what we may have to go through or the pain we may have to experience along the way, but we do know if we lean on God and allow Him to help us be the people He sees, we will be blessed because God will get the glory out of the suffering. It will all work together for good.

Know that God is doing something behind the scenes. We have to trust the process and know that Jeremiah 18: 4-6, says, "He was making a pot from clay. But there was something wrong with the pot. So the potter used the clay to make another pot. With his hands he shaped the pot the way he wanted it to be." Then he said, "Family of Israel, you know that I can do the same thing with you. You are like the clay in the potter's hands, and I am the potter." You see, unless we are willing to allow God to make and mode us so we can change, we will be stuck in our pain. He has your back, and if you feel you can't go any further, that's when you know God is pushing you through, so don't give up. I now can accept my calling because he called me at 23 years old and I was afraid to do his will due to my feeling that I was worthless. He gave me Jeremiah 1: 1-10 because he called me from my mother's womb I remember crying. God knew me before I knew myself and I ran from him because I didn't feel that I was qualified, but he qualified me to be a Prophetess, and Evangelist and Preacher. I now hold my head up and know who I am in Christ and you can too. You don't have

Pushing Through The Pain

to let pain defeat you but you can go through knowing that God will bring you out and it takes trials and tribulation, it takes testing of your faith to know that God is with you and believe in yourself. You have to be tested, remember Jesus was tested in the wilderness, and you will be too.

Let's pray say this to God: God I thank you for all of my trials, I know that you will bring me out help me to be more grateful and thankful so that my attitude is pleasing in your sight. Help me to love the way you love and love myself so that I can love someone else. Help me to accept that even though I didn't deserve your love that you love me and no one can compare to your love. I thank you that all that will live Godly in Christ Jesus shall suffer persecution. 2 Corinthians 12:10. I am a willing vessel help me to let your will be done in my life . I surrender unto you in the name of Jesus I pray Amen.

www.ingramcontent.com/pod-product-compliance
Lightning Source LLC
LaVergne TN
LVHW051954060526
838201LV00059B/3649